DELTA
YOUNG LEARNERS ENGLISH

Fantastic Flyers

An activity-based course for young learners

Pupil's Book

Viv Lambert and Cheryl Pelteret

Fantastic Flyers

DELTA Publishing
Quince Cottage
Hoe Lane
Peaslake
Surrey GU5 9SW
United Kingdom

Email: fantasticflyers@deltapublishing.co.uk
www.deltapublishing.co.uk

First published 2008

Project managed by Chris Hartley
Edited by Barbara MacKay
Designed by Peter Bushell
Illustrations by Philip Bannister, Geo Parkin, Alek Sotirovski and Ian West
Photographs by Michael Little Photography
Picture Research by Mandy Twells
Printed by Halstan & Co, Amersham, UK

ISBN: 978 1 905085 09 5

Contents

Around the world

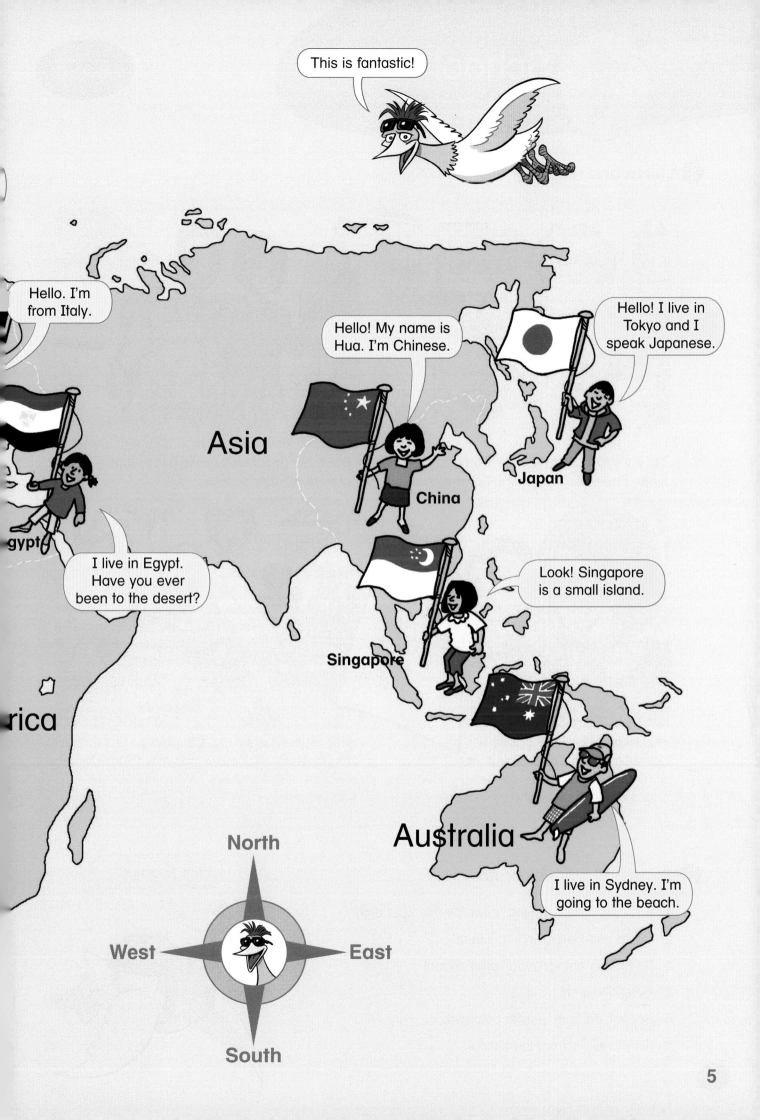

5

1 Listen and read 🎧 1

Hi! I'm Robert. I take the bus to school. I'm early today. It's twenty-five past eight. The bus comes at half past eight.

Hello! I'm David. I walk to school with my sister, Helen. My rucksack's really heavy today. I've got football after school.

TIMETABLE
8.45 - Art
9.15 - History

Hi, I'm Helen. We've got art at school today. Art is my favourite subject. After art we've got history. Hurry up, David! School starts at quarter to nine.

Hello. My name's Katy. It's twenty to nine, but I'm still at home. I'm not going to be late for school. It isn't far. I live next to the school. See you later!

2 Read and say *yes* or *no*

1 Robert's bus is coming at twenty-five past eight.

2 David and Helen walk to school.

3 David has got volleyball after school.

4 Helen likes art.

5 School starts at quarter past nine.

6 Katy lives far from the school.

I fly to school!

1 Complete the sentences

1 Robert takes ....

2 The bus comes at ....

3 David has got football ....

4 School starts at ....

5 Katy lives ....

6 She isn't going to be ....

2 Listen and order the cards 🎧 2

➡ Teacher's Book page P2

3 Ask and answer together

1 What lessons have we got today?

2 What's your favourite subject?

3 Do you like art?

4 How do you get to school?

5 Which languages do you study?

1 **Look and listen. Then answer.** 🎧 3

1 What time is it?

2 When does lunchtime finish?

3 What's Emma doing?

4 What's William doing?

5 What are Sarah and Michael doing?

2 **Memory game. Work with a partner.**
Partner A, close your book. Partner B, ask questions.

1 Read and order the pictures

We had art at school today, but we didn't go to the art classroom. We went on a bus to town and we visited the museum. We looked at paintings by famous artists and we found out about them.

My favourite painting was by Picasso. It was very strange. After we looked at the paintings we made pictures for a competition. I drew my teacher. My picture looked like a Picasso painting. My teacher wasn't very pleased, so I didn't win!

2 Choose the best title

A visit to the art museum

An interesting artist

My art teacher

3 Do it together

➡ Teacher's Book page P3

What's Katy's teacher's name?

Mr Brown.

1 **Look at picture A and answer the questions**

1 Which room is this?
2 What time is it?
3 How many books are there?
4 What's the boy doing?
5 What colour is the blanket?
6 What's on the floor?

2 **Look at picture B and say the differences**

In picture A, it's four o'clock.
In picture B, it's half past four.

3 **Guessing game**

Are you eating breakfast?

No.

Are you eating lunch?

Yes.

Is it half past twelve?

Yes.

1 **Talk about the pictures**

An interesting lesson

2 **Answer the questions**

1 What subject are they studying?

2 Did David go to bed early last night?

3 What does David do at quarter to ten?

4 What time does the lesson end?

5 What do you think the teacher says?

3 **Continue the story**

It's half past nine in the morning. David is at school. They're studying …

1 Listen, point and say 🎧 4

singing

actors

theatre

famous

television

2 Read and choose the correct word from above

Do you want to be on **1** .... ?

Do you want to be famous?

You should go to theatre school. These schools look like other

schools. They teach languages, maths, science and the other

subjects, but the students also study **2** ....,

dancing and acting. After they leave school, many students

get jobs in television or **3** .... Some students

are **4** .... or singers. Only a few are

5 ....

I want to be famous

3 Read and choose the correct words

1 Theatre schools look **like/as** other schools.

2 They teach **many/a few** subjects.

3 Students also **study/studying** singing.

4 They get jobs in television **before/after** they leave school.

5 **Many/Some** students are actors or singers.

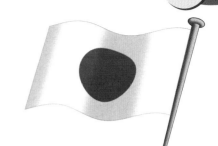

① **Read and find out. Answer the questions.**

1 Where is Hiro?

2 Does he like school?

3 Does he go home for lunch?

Flying visit: Japan

Name: Hiro
Age: 13
Country: Japan

Hello! My name's Hiro and I'm from Japan. This is my school. We go to school by car. School starts at half past eight and finishes at three o'clock, but we don't go home. After school, we go to clubs and do more lessons, sports, art and music.

I like my school. The classrooms are very big and there are no walls so we have to work quietly.

At lunchtime we have chicken, soup and rice. We don't use knives and forks. We use chopsticks. After lunch we clean the classrooms and the toilets. We work together in teams so it's good fun.

We have playtime twice a day for 25 minutes, one in the morning and one in the afternoon. We play outside in the playground or we stay inside and read books or use the computers.

② **Make sentences about Hiro and his school**

1 He goes to school by …

2 School starts …

3 After school, he …

4 At lunchtime, he uses …

5 At playtime, he …

How do you go to school?

1 **Listen and read** 🎧 5

It was winter. One Saturday morning in December when David and Helen woke up, the garden was white. 'It's snowing!' they shouted. 'Let's put on our warm clothes and go out in the snow.'

'Let's make a snowman!' They made two big snowballs for his body and his head. Helen cut some card for his nose. David found two pieces of glass for his eyes. They found a piece of wood for his mouth. 'He needs clothes!' said David. David took off his striped scarf. Katy took off her gloves and hat, and David gave the snowman his coat and belt.

'Look, Mum!' said Helen. 'Look at our snowman. His eyes are made of glass, his nose is made of card, his mouth is made of wood and his clothes are made of wool. He's nice and warm now!'

'Yes, he is, but *you* aren't!' said Mum. 'Come inside and sit by the fire.'

2 **Read and say *yes* or *no***

1 It was spring.

2 David and Helen were excited when they saw the snow.

3 They made two big snowmen.

4 The snowman's eyes were made of glass.

5 The snowman wore David's gloves.

6 Mum told them to stay outside.

It's cold outside!

1 Complete the sentences

I'm making a snowman.

1 It wasn't summer, it was ....

2 David and Helen put on their ....

3 They made a ....

4 His nose was ....

5 David gave the snowman ....

6 After they made the snowman, they ....

2 Listen and match the months to the children 6 → Teacher's Book page P4

Betty

Richard

Sarah

Michael

3 Ask and answer together

1 What date is it today?

2 Is your birthday in winter?

3 What's your favourite month?

4 Do you like snow?

5 Which do you like best: summer, winter, spring or autumn?

What date is it today?

It's the first of November.

1 **Look and listen. Then answer.** 🎧 7

1 What month is it?
2 What are they doing?
3 What's Emma wearing?
4 What are Michael and William doing?
5 What does Richard love?

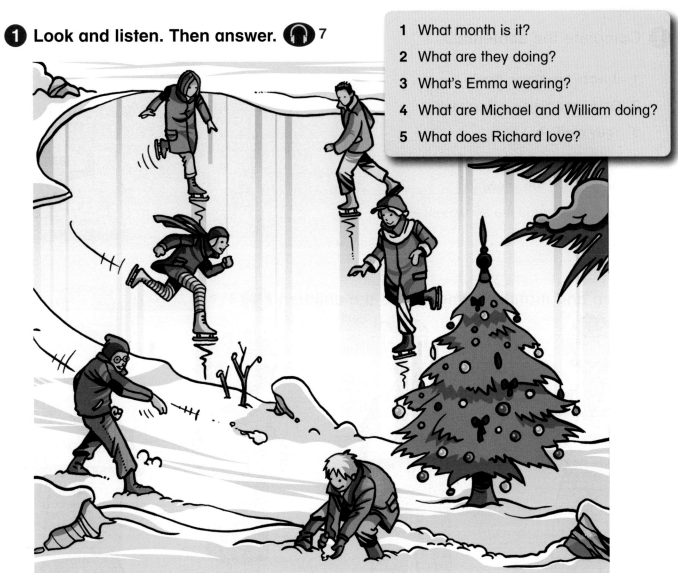

2 **Memory game. Work with a partner.**
Partner A, close your book. Partner B, ask questions.

Which...?

What's the weather like?

Where...?

It's cold and foggy.

What...?

What colour...?

How many...?

Who...?

1 Read and order the pictures

Last winter, our school closed for one day when it snowed.

We were so excited. My brother and I went home and we made a sledge from card and string. Then we went to the park. There were lots of children there with different sledges. Some were made of wood or plastic, others were made of metal.

'Shall we have a race?' suggested one boy. Some children laughed when they saw our sledge. 'You aren't going to win with that sledge! It's going to break!' shouted one boy. We went to the top of the hill and we all sledged down.

Some children fell off. It was funny. Can you guess who won? Yes, we won! Our sledge looked funny but it was the best!

2 Choose the best title

At the park

Our school in winter

The sledge race

3 Do it together

➡ Teacher's Book page P5

Which month is it?

It's January.

1 Look at picture A and answer the questions

1 Which month is it?

2 Is it summer or winter?

3 How many people are there?

4 What does the woman want to buy?

5 What's the weather like?

6 What's the man who's wearing a black coat doing?

2 Look at picture B and say the differences

In picture A, it's winter.
In picture B, it's summer.

3 Birthday survey

➡ Teacher's Book page P6

When's your birthday?

It's in May.

LESSON 6

1 Talk about the pictures

A storm in the hills

2 Answer the questions

1 Where were the children?

2 What was the weather like?

3 Where did they go when there was a storm?

4 What did they do in this place?

5 How did they get home?

3 Continue the story

One afternoon in autumn, Sarah and three friends walked in the hills. There were black clouds ...

1 **Listen, point and say**  8

boat

beach

belt

midday

storms

2 **Read and choose the correct word from above**

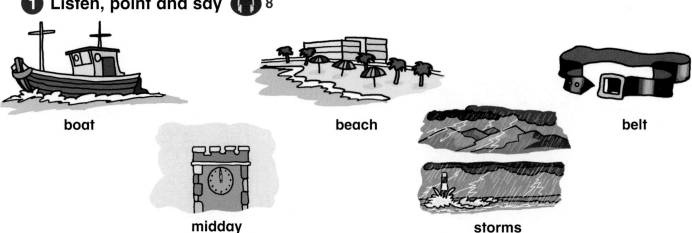

Christmas in Australia is usually very hot. Sometimes there are **1** ...., but it never snows. It's in December but it isn't in winter, it's in summer. People often have a picnic at **2** .... by the swimming pool or they eat Christmas dinner on the **3** .... They wear shorts and T-shirts and Father Christmas arrives by **4** .... He wears a red hat and a red coat with a black **5** .... and black boots. He must be very hot!

3 **Read and choose the correct words**

1 Christmas in Australia is in **winter/summer.**

2 People usually eat **inside/outside.**

3 They **wear/wearing** shorts and T-shirts.

4 Father Christmas arrives **in/by** boat.

5 His clothes **make/makes** him very hot.

Merry Christmas!

1 Read and find out. Answer the questions.

1 What season is it?
2 What are the people doing in the photo?
3 What do you think the hotel is made of?

Flying visit: Canada

Name: Carrie
Age: 12
Country: Canada

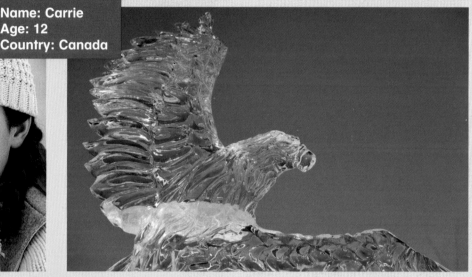

My name's Carrie and I'm from Canada. In February in my country it's very cold and it snows. We have the biggest winter party in the world. A big friendly snowman says 'hello' when you arrive.

There's a football game in the snow, there are sledge races and there's a boat race across the river. Sometimes there is ice on the river. It's very difficult and very funny!

People come from all over the world. Some people stay in the ice hotel. The walls are made of ice and the beds are made of ice. It's very cold. They have to build a new hotel every winter.

Artists build animals and people made of snow. There is a competition for the best snowman. I like this bird made of ice. It's beautiful.

2 Make sentences about winter in Carrie's country

1 In February …
2 They have the biggest …
3 There is a boat race …
4 Some people stay in …
5 Carrie likes …

What do you do in winter?

① Listen and read 🎧 9

David is going to stay at Robert's house at the weekend. He's getting ready now. He's very excited. He's going to sleep in Robert's room.

He's putting a torch and some books in his suitcase. They're going to read books and tell stories until late. He's got some toys and computer games. He's taking sweets and biscuits, too. They're going to have a snack at midnight. They aren't going to tell Helen.

David's suitcase is heavy. 'David,' says his mum, 'what have you got in your suitcase? You're only going to stay for one night!'

'I know,' says David, 'but we're going to do lots of things together.'

'Shall I put your comb, your soap and your toothbrush in your bag?' asks his mum.

'I'm not going to wash!' says David. 'We're going to be too busy.'

'You *are* going to wash and you *are* going to brush your teeth,' says David's mum, 'or you *aren't* going to go!'

② Read and say *yes* or *no*

1 David's going to sleep in Robert's room.

2 They're going to go to bed early.

3 They're going to eat biscuits and sweets at midnight.

4 David's suitcase is light.

5 He's going to stay for two nights.

6 David's comb is in his suitcase.

David's going to be tired.

LESSON 2

1 Complete the sentences

1 David's going to stay ....

2 He's taking some books because ....

3 They're going to .... at midnight.

4 They aren't going ....

5 David's suitcase ....

6 David says he isn't ....

I'm going to come, too!

2 Listen and order the cards 🎧 10

→ Teacher's Book page P7

3 Ask and answer together

1 What are you going to do in the holidays?

2 How are you going to get there?

3 What are you going to take?

4 Are you going to take a rucksack?

5 Are you going to send any postcards?

What are you going to do in the holidays?

I'm going to stay with my grandparents.

1 **Look and listen. Then answer.** 🎧 11

1   What's this place?

2   What's everyone going to do?

3   What's the woman in the bookshop going to buy?

4   What's the man outside the toilet going to do?

5   What's the boy with the rucksack doing?

2 **Memory game. Work with a partner.**
Partner A, close your book. Partner B, ask questions.

1 Read and order the pictures

Last Sunday, my dad went to London on business. He went by plane and he wore a pair of jeans and a T-shirt.

When he arrived at the airport in London, he waited for his suitcase. He saw a blue suitcase that looked like his suitcase and he picked it up. Then he took a taxi to his hotel. He was very tired and he went to bed.

The next morning he got up and opened his suitcase. It was full of women's clothes!

He had to go to his meeting in his jeans and T-shirt!

2 Choose the best title

A holiday in London

The wrong suitcase

An interesting meeting

3 Do it together

➡ Teacher's Book page P8

Where's Katy going to go?

She's going to go to the country.

1 Look at picture A and answer the questions

1 Is it summer or winter?

2 What are the children doing?

3 What are they going to do?

4 How many people are outside the hotel?

5 What are they going to do?

6 What are the people under the trees doing?

2 Look at picture B and say the differences

> In picture A, three children are going to swim. In picture B, two children are going to swim.

3 Chain game

> I'm going to go on holiday and I'm going to take a camera.

> I'm going to go on holiday and I'm going to take a camera and some money.

1 Talk about the pictures

A camping holiday

2 Answer the questions

1 What was the weather like?

2 Where did they sleep?

3 What happened during the night?

4 How did they feel in the morning?

5 Where are they going to stay next time?

3 Continue the story

David and his family went on a camping holiday. The weather was …

1 Listen, point and say 🎧 12

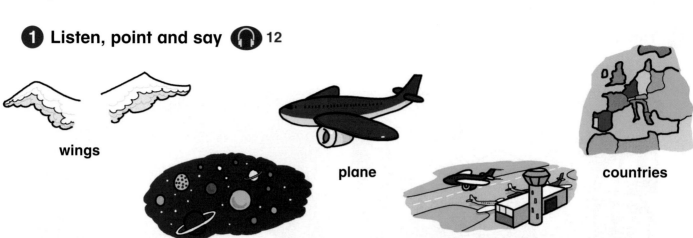

wings

space

plane

airport

countries

2 Read and choose the correct word from above

About 100 years ago the Wright brothers made the first **1** ....

They watched birds flying and studied their **2** .... Their plane was made of wood and the wings were made of cloth, like our clothes. They flew from a field. There wasn't an **3** ....

Today big, metal planes carry hundreds of people to **4** .... all over the world and rockets fly into **5** .... But is flying good for the environment?

3 Read and choose the correct words

1 Two brothers made the first **airport/plane**.

2 They studied birds' **wings/feet**.

3 Their plane was made of **wood and metal/wood and cloth**.

4 There **were many/weren't any** airports.

5 Flying **is/isn't** good for the environment.

Flying is easy!

1 **Read and find out. Answer the questions.**

1 Where is Austin going to go?

2 Who is going to be there?

3 Name three things he is going to do.

Flying visit: USA

Hi, my name's Austin and I'm getting ready to go to summer camp. I'm going to stay for three weeks without Mom and Dad! It's OK. There are adults there too and lots of other children. People come from all over the world to look after the children at summer camp.

This summer camp is in the countryside in a forest. There's a lake and around the lake there are lots of small houses made of wood. I'm going to sleep in one of these houses with some other children.

Name: Austin
Age: 13
Country: USA

We're going to do different things. We're going to ride bikes in the forest, go horse riding and take boats out on the lake. We're going to play tennis, basketball and baseball. We're also going to paint pictures and make things.

In the evenings, we're going to cook dinner over a fire. We're going to tell stories and sing songs. I'm going to enjoy summer camp. I'm going to have fun, make new friends and try new things.

2 **Make sentences about Austin and his holiday**

1 He's going to stay at summer camp for …

2 This summer camp is in …

3 He's going to sleep in …

4 In the day, he's going to …

5 In the evening, he's going to …

Talk about your next holiday.

29

1 Listen and read 🎧 13

One day, David took his tape recorder to school. At lunchtime he walked around the playground asking lots of questions. First, he turned on the tape recorder and he asked Robert, 'Robert, what do you want to do when you leave school?' Robert replied, 'I'm going to be a footballer. I'm going to play for my town. I'm going to wear a blue and white striped shirt …'

'OK, thank you,' said David. Then he asked the same question to Harry. 'I'm going to go to college,' said Harry. 'I want to be an actor. I'm not going to work in the theatre. I'm going to be on television. I'm going to be famous!'

'Very interesting,' said David. Then he saw Katy on the swing. He asked, 'What are you going to do when you leave school, Katy?'

'I want to work in a circus,' she said. 'I'm going to be a clown. I'm going to have orange hair and a big, red nose. I'm going to make people laugh.'

David laughed. 'That's great. Thank you,' he said. He turned the tape recorder off and started to write in a book.

'What are you doing?' asked Katy. 'Why are you asking so many questions?'

'I'm trying to find out which jobs children want to do,' said David. 'I'm going to write about it and send it to the newspaper. I want to be a journalist when I leave school.'

2 Read and say *yes* or *no*

1 Robert wants to be a footballer.

2 Harry's going to go to university.

3 Harry wants to work in the theatre.

4 Katy's going to work in an office.

5 Katy's going to make people laugh.

6 David wants to be a doctor.

I want to be a pilot.

UNIT 4

1 Complete the sentences

1 David turned ....

2 Robert's going to wear ....

3 David asked the same ....

4 Katy wants to work ....

5 She's going to make ....

6 David's trying to find ....

I want to work in a circus.

2 Listen and order the cards 14

→ Teacher's Book page P9

3 Ask and answer together

1 What does your dad do?

2 What does your mum do?

3 What do you want to do when you leave school?

4 Are you going to wear a uniform?

5 Do you want to make people laugh?

What does your dad do?

He's a businessman.

1 Look and listen. Then answer. 🎧 15

1 What happened at the factory?

2 Who's in the ambulance?

3 What's the journalist doing now?

4 What's he going to do?

5 What's the photographer going to do?

2 Memory game. Work with a partner.
Partner A, close your book. Partner B, ask questions.

Why...?

Who's in front of the ambulance?

Where...?

What...?

What colour...?

The journalist.

How many...?

Who...?

1 Read and order the pictures

Last Saturday, it was my mum's 40th birthday. We went to an expensive restaurant for dinner.

The waiter was very excited because there was a famous actress in the restaurant. She was with her husband.

I walked past their table on my way to the toilet. Suddenly a photographer arrived and started taking photos.

The next day the photo was in the newspaper – the actress, her husband and me! I always wanted to be famous!

2 Choose the best title

Famous for one day

An expensive meal

A great photo

3 Do it together

Teacher's Book page P10

What does Harry's dad do?

He's a pilot.

1 **Look at picture A and answer the questions**

1 Where are these people?

2 What time is it?

3 How many people are there?

4 What's the boy eating?

5 What colour is the paint?

6 What's the waiter carrying?

2 **Look at picture B and say the differences**

In picture A, the waiter is carrying three full glasses. In picture B, he's carrying three empty glasses.

3 **Guessing game**

Do you work inside?

No.

Do you wear a uniform?

Yes.

LESSON 6

1 **Talk about the pictures**

At the theatre

STAGE DOOR

2 **Answer the questions**

1 Where did Katy go?

2 Did she enjoy it?

3 Why did she wait at the theatre door?

4 Where did she ask the man to write his name?

5 Why did the man laugh?

3 **Continue the story**

Katy went to the theatre with her parents. They enjoyed …

1 Listen, point and say 🎧 16

office

journalist

newspaper

telephone

photographers

2 Read and choose the correct word from above

Do you want to be a newspaper **1** ....?
It's an interesting job. You have to be good at writing
stories and you have to write quickly. The newspaper
2 .... is very noisy. There are lots of
people talking on the **3** .... News
happens all over the world in the day and night.
4 .... bring in their photos and people
work during the night to get the **5** ....
ready for the next morning.

3 Read and choose the correct words

1 Journalists have to be good at **write/writing** stories.

2 They have to write **quietly/quickly.**

3 News happens **in the office/all over the world.**

4 The newspaper office is **noisy/quiet.**

5 People work **at night/in the morning** to get the
newspaper ready.

Is it a bird?

LESSON 8

1 Read and find out. Answer the questions.

1 How many brothers and sisters has Esi got?
2 Where do her parents work?
3 Does she help them?

Flying visit: Ghana

Hello! My name's Esi and this is my mum. We're from Ghana in Africa. We're farmers. We live on a farm in a village. We grow cocoa trees on our farm. Chocolate is made from cocoa beans. Do you like chocolate?

My mum and dad work on the farm all day. My brother and sister and I go to school. We study maths, history and English. In the afternoon, we play outside together and we help Mum and Dad on the farm.

**Name: Esi
Age: 11
Country:
Ghana**

When the cocoa fruit is ready, we help to pick the fruit. The beans are inside the green fruit. We take the beans and put them in the sun to dry.

When the beans are dry we put them in big bags and our parents take them to the market. They sell the beans at the market and then they come home. They're tired, but everybody is happy.

2 Make sentences about Esi and her farm

1 Esi lives …
2 They grow …
3 The children go to school and study …
4 In the afternoon they …
5 They sell the beans at …

Do you like chocolate?

1 Listen and read 🎧 17

Last Saturday, Katy had nothing to do. 'I'm bored,' she said. There were some holiday magazines next to her and she picked one up and started to read it. 'That's it!' she said. 'I'm going to plan a holiday. I want to do something new and exciting.'

Her friends came to her house. 'What are you doing, Katy?' they asked.

'I'm planning an exciting holiday,' she explained. 'I want to do something different.'

David opened a magazine. 'Have you ever ridden a camel across the desert?' he asked.

'No, I haven't,' answered Katy. 'But the desert is too hot.'

Robert took another magazine. 'Have you ever been skiing in the mountains?' he asked.

'Yes, I have,' said Katy. 'We went last year. I was too cold. I wasn't warm enough.'

'Have you ever eaten octopus in a restaurant by the sea?' asked Helen.

'No, I haven't,' said Katy. 'I prefer my mum's cooking.'

'Are you sure you want to do something new and exciting?' asked David.

'No,' said Katy. 'I'm not bored any more. This is fun!'

2 Read and say *yes* or *no*

1 Last Saturday, Katy was bored.

2 Katy has ridden a camel across the desert.

3 Katy hasn't been skiing.

4 She likes skiing.

5 She hasn't eaten octopus.

6 Katy doesn't want to do something new and exciting.

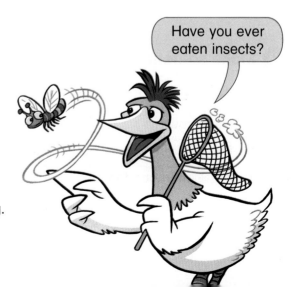

Have you ever eaten insects?

LESSON 2

1 Complete the sentences

1 Katy wanted to do something ....

2 David asked, 'Have you .... ?'

3 Last year Katy went ....

4 She wasn't warm ....

5 Helen asked, 'Have you .... octopus?'

6 Katy prefers ....

I've never skied before.

2 Match the cards. Then listen and order. 🎧 18

➡ Teacher's Book page P11

ride **ridden** **eat** **eaten**

have **had**

3 Ask and answer together

1 Have you ever ridden a camel?

2 Have you ever been to the desert?

3 Where did you go on holiday last year?

4 Did you take any photos?

5 What's the best holiday you've ever had?

Have you ever ridden a camel?

No, I haven't.

1 **Look and listen. Then answer.** 🎧 19

1 Why is the little girl crying?

2 What have the two boys at the shop just done?

3 Why is the little boy angry?

4 Who has just jumped in the pool?

5 How many postcards has the woman written?

2 **Memory game. Work with a partner.**
Partner A, close your book. Partner B, ask questions.

Why...?

What's the little girl who has just dropped her ice cream wearing?

Where...?

What...?

What colour...?

How many...?

Who...?

She's wearing green shorts and a yellow T-shirt.

1 Read and order the pictures

Tom is on his way to school. It starts to rain. 'Oh, no,' he says, 'I've forgotten my coat.'

He walks back home and gets his coat. He's half way to school when he stops because he's left his lunch at home. He goes back home again.

'This time I've got everything,' he says, but he hasn't got everything. He's forgotten his rucksack. When he gets home his brother is having breakfast.

'Have you forgotten something?' his brother asks. 'My rucksack?' says Tom. 'No,' says his brother. 'You've forgotten the date. It's Saturday the 12th of November. It's the weekend. There's no school today!'

2 Choose the best title

Back to school

An interesting day

Have you forgotten something?

3 Do it together

→ Teacher's Book page P12

How old are William's grandparents?

His grandpa is 80 and his grandma is 72.

1 Look at picture A and answer the questions

1 How many children have already finished their paintings?

2 Has the boy with glasses finished his painting yet?

3 Is the classroom tidy or untidy?

4 What has the boy with glasses just done?

5 What has the teacher just done?

6 How do you think the teacher feels?

2 Look at picture B and say the differences

In picture A, a boy has dropped the paint. In picture B, he's picked it up.

3 Play a game

➡ Teacher's Book page P13

Snap!

① Talk about the pictures

The naughty puppy

② Answer the questions

1 What does Helen get for her birthday?

2 Who comes to Helen's house?

3 What presents do they bring?

4 Where is the puppy when they go into the kitchen?

5 What has the puppy done?

③ Continue the story

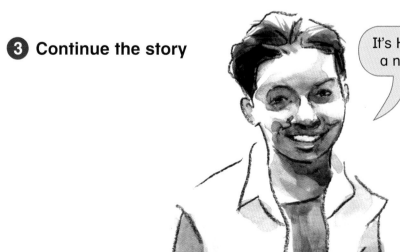

It's Helen's birthday. She's got a new puppy. Her friends …

1 Listen, point and say 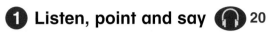 20

fog

helicopter

ice

air

mountains

2 Read and choose the correct word from above

Alan Hinkes has climbed the fourteen highest

1 .... in the world. Climbing these high

mountains is very dangerous. People can only live for a few

days in the thin **2** ....

Alan has fallen many times on the **3** ....

Once he hurt his back badly and walked through the

4 .... for ten days before a

5 .... found him and took him to hospital.

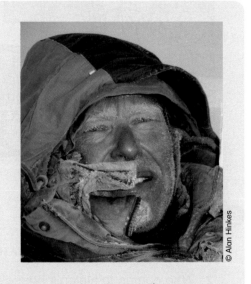

© Alan Hinkes

Alan is also a very good photographer. He has made films and written books about climbing.

He wants to climb more mountains and he wants to write more books.

3 Read and choose the correct words

1 Alan Hinkes **climbed/has climbed** the highest mountains.

2 He **has fallen/fell** many times.

3 In 1997 he **hurt/has hurt** his back badly.

4 A helicopter found him **before/after** he walked for ten days through the fog.

5 Alan **wrote/has written** books about climbing.

LESSON 8

1 Read and find out. Answer the questions.

1 Does Ali live in the city?

2 What can you find in the desert?

3 What is the name of the sea near Ali's country?

Flying visit: Egypt

Name: Ali
Age: 11
Country: Egypt

My name's Ali and I live near the desert in Egypt. Have you ever been to the desert? It's very hot and dry in my country but there are lots of things to see and do. There are busy cities, mountains, rivers and beaches. It's a great place for a holiday.

You can stay in a hotel in the city for a few days. You can shop at the markets and eat out in different restaurants every night. The food is excellent.

Many people visit my country. They come from all over the world to see the pyramids. Have you heard about the pyramids? You can ride a camel across the desert and camp in a tent. I've ridden a camel many times and I've seen the pyramids. They look very beautiful in the evening sun.

Have you ever dreamed of swimming with dolphins? I've swum with dolphins in the Red Sea. It's great! There are lots of strange and lovely fish, too. So, when are you going to visit me?

2 Make sentences about Ali and his country

1 The weather in his country is …

2 There are mountains, …

3 In the city you can …

4 People visit his country because they want to see …

5 He has …

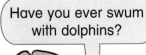

Have you ever swum with dolphins?

1 Listen and read 🎧 21

On Saturday night, Mum was cooking dinner in the kitchen. David and Helen were watching an exciting TV programme about two children.

The children were on holiday. One evening, they got lost in the woods. A light was shining in the trees. It was a castle!

'We might meet a queen or a king!' the children thought. 'Perhaps they could help us get home.'

As they were pushing their bikes up the hill, they saw an envelope on a tree. Inside, there was a gold ring and a letter. The letter said, 'You have the queen's missing ring. Go to the castle. Look for the key. It's in a secret place. If you find the key, open the door. Your present is inside the castle.'

Then the TV programme ended.

'Do you think they are going to find the key?' asked Helen.

'I don't know,' said David. 'Hey, what's this?' He felt something hard on the sofa. It was a key!

'This is strange!' Helen whispered to David. 'We've found the secret key!'

Mum came into the room. 'Has anyone seen my key? I lost it this morning …'

David laughed. 'Sorry, Helen. I don't think this is the secret key!'

2 Read and say *yes* or *no*

1 David and Helen were watching TV with their mother.
2 They were having dinner.
3 The programme they were watching was boring.
4 The programme was about a family.
5 They didn't find out how the story ended.
6 Mum's missing key was lying on the sofa.

Where's the secret key?

I think they're going to find the key.

1 Complete the sentences

1 David and Helen's mother .... dinner.

2 David and Helen .... TV.

3 In the story, two children .... one evening.

4 They saw an envelope ....

5 There was .... inside the envelope.

6 David found .... on the sofa.

2 Listen and order the cards 🎧 22

→ Teacher's Book page P14

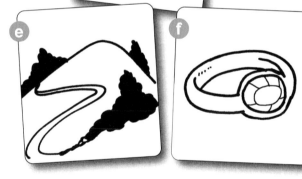

What famous place have you visited?

3 Ask and answer together

1 What famous place have you visited?

2 Where is it?

3 What was the weather like when you went there?

4 What did you see there?

5 What did you buy?

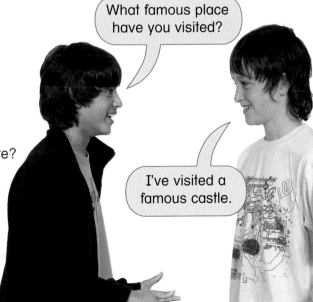

I've visited a famous castle.

1 **Look and listen. Then answer.** 🎧 23

1 What's in the envelope?

2 Who's reading about the competition?

3 What can she win in the competition?

4 What are the three secret things in the picture?

5 Who lives in the castle?

2 **Memory game. Work with a partner.**
Partner A, close your book. Partner B, ask questions.

Why...?

What colour is the queen's dress?

Where...?

What...?

It's red.

What colour...?

How many...?

Who...?

1 Read and order the pictures

On 5th December, 1872, some people were sailing on a boat. They saw a ship near them. The wind was blowing, but the ship wasn't moving. They couldn't see any people on the ship. They went nearer the ship. Then they saw the name: *Mary Celeste*.

'That's strange,' the people said. 'It looks empty. Perhaps something has happened. Let's help.'

So they climbed on to the ship. There was no-one there. A diary was lying on the desk. The last date in the diary was 24th November!

What happened to the people on the *Mary Celeste*? There are lots of strange stories about the ship. People say, 'In the kitchen, food was cooking on the cooker. The table was ready for a meal: knives, forks and spoons were lying on the table. It looked like the people were having breakfast. There was a cat sleeping on the chair.' Do you think these stories are true? Read about the *Mary Celeste* and find out!

2 Choose the best title

The year 1872

The strange story of the *Mary Celeste*

The last date in the diary

3 Do it together

➡ Teacher's Book page P15

When did it happen?

It happened in 1864.

UNIT 6

LESSON 5

1 **Look at picture A and answer the questions**

1. What was the weather like at 12.30 p.m.?

2. What was the boy doing?

3. What was the girl eating?

4. What were the children's parents doing?

5. What were the other people at the hotel doing?

12.30 p.m.

2 **Look at picture B and say the differences**

B 12.45 p.m.

HOTEL

At 12.30 p.m., it was sunny.
At 12.45 p.m., it was raining.

3 **Finding out game**

➡ Teacher's Book page P16

What were you doing on Saturday afternoon at three o'clock?

I was playing football.

① Talk about the pictures

At Robert's grandparents' house

Perhaps it's a secret way to the castle.

② Answer the questions

1 Where were Harry and Robert playing?

2 What happened to the ball?

3 What did they find while they were looking for the ball?

4 Why did they go down the stairs?

5 Did the stairs go to the castle?

③ Continue the story

Harry and Robert were visiting Robert's grandfather's house. One day, they were …

1 Listen, point and say 🎧 24

queen

cook

king

lamps

fire

2 Read and choose the correct word from above

Life in a castle long ago wasn't always easy. Castles were cold places, with only a

1 .... and blankets to keep you warm. They were dark, too, with only

2 .... for light.

The most important people in the castle were the **3** .... and his wife, the **4** .... But there were a lot of people who worked for them and their family. Working in a castle was a hard job. There was so much to do! While the **5** .... was making dinner, other workers were washing clothes and tidying the rooms.

Castles weren't quiet places. They didn't always smell nice, because there were lots of animals inside the building!

I'm the king of the castle.

3 Read and choose the correct words

1 Living in a castle **was/wasn't** often hard.

2 There **were/weren't** blankets to keep you warm.

3 People had **fires/lamps** for light.

4 The **cook/king and queen** had to make the dinner.

5 Castles were **noisy/quiet** places.

1 Read and find out. Answer the questions.

1 Where is Michael's favourite place?

2 Name a king and a queen who lived there.

3 What can you see there today?

Flying visit: England

Name: Michael
Age: 12
Country: England

My name's Michael. I live in London. This is a picture of my favourite place to visit, the Tower of London. Today it's a museum, but for many centuries, kings lived there.

King Henry III was the first king who lived there, in 1240. Many people visited him from all over the world, and they brought him animals as presents. He made a lake around the building, with a bridge over it. Near the bridge, he made a zoo. He had lots of lions and camels there. Visitors could see and hear them, when they arrived at the gates.

Many terrible things happened in this place, too. King Henry VIII's second wife died here. Her name was Queen Anne Boleyn. The king cut off her head. After she died, some people said they could still see her. She was walking around and carrying her head under her arm. Do you think this story is true?

Today, people can see some of Britain's famous treasure here. One of the treasures is King William IV's gold ring.

2 Make sentences about Michael's favourite place

1 Michael's favourite place is …

2 Many years ago …

3 King Henry III made …

4 He had …

5 Today, you can see …

What's your favourite place?

1 Listen and read 🎧 25

Harry and Katy were hungry.

'Here, have a few of my sweets,' said Harry.

'No, thank you,' said Katy. 'You shouldn't eat so many sweets. They're bad for your teeth.'

They went into the kitchen. They wanted to make a snack to eat. Harry saw a plate of chocolate biscuits. 'Let's have a few each!' said Harry. But Katy said, 'Biscuits are full of butter and flour, aren't they? And they're full of sugar, too. Too much sugar isn't good for you, is it? What about a salad?'

They opened the fridge. Katy was looking for some tomatoes or vegetables. But Harry found some pizza. 'It's got cheese and tomatoes on it ... so it's very healthy!' said Harry.

'No, Harry. Pizza isn't a snack. It's a meal!' said Katy. 'If you want a snack, eat apples or other fruit.'

Later ...

Harry came into the kitchen. Katy was eating ice cream with biscuits and chocolate on top. 'That isn't a healthy snack, is it?' said Harry.

'But I'm only having a little ice cream,' said Katy, 'and it tastes very nice!'

2 Read and say *yes* or *no*

1 There's a lot of salt in sweets.

2 A lot of sugar is good for you.

3 Biscuits have got a lot of sugar in them.

4 There is flour, sugar and butter in a salad.

5 Fruit is a healthy snack.

Too many biscuits aren't good for you!

I eat lots of fruit.

1 Complete the sentences

1 Harry wants Katy to eat ....

2 Harry saw a plate of ....

3 .... isn't good for you, is it?

4 Harry's pizza has got .... , hasn't it?

5 Katy decides to have ....

2 Listen and order the cards 🎧 26

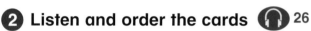

➡ Teacher's Book page P17

3 Ask and answer together

1 Harry likes pizza, doesn't he?

2 Biscuits are full of sugar, aren't they?

3 Sweets aren't good for your teeth, are they?

4 Too much salt is bad for you, isn't it?

5 You don't eat lots of sugar, do you?

Harry likes pizza, doesn't he?

Yes, he does.

1 **Look and listen. Then answer.** 🎧 27

1 What is this place?

2 What are the children and their father going to eat?

3 What is their mother going to eat her meal with?

4 What is the boy going to eat before his meal?

5 What should they all do before they put salt and pepper on their food?

2 **Memory game. Work with a partner.**
Partner A, close your book. Partner B, ask questions.

Why...?

How many plates is the waiter carrying?

Where...?

What...?

Three.

What colour...?

How many...?

Who...?

1 Read and order the pictures

A funny thing happened to my friend and me last week. We were shopping at the market. We saw a table with lots of different kinds of fruit on it – apples, mangoes, bananas, pears. We saw a few people smelling the fruit. I picked up a mango and smelled it. It smelled really nice. Then I saw a card next to it. It said, 'Try a little!'

'OK, I'll try it,' I thought.

I put it in my mouth. Just then, my friend shouted, 'Stop, Richard! This isn't fruit!

'But it looks like a mango and it smells like a mango,' I said.

'But it doesn't feel like a mango, and it doesn't taste like a mango,' said my friend.

'How do you know?' I asked.

'Because it's soap! Look! You can't eat it, or any of them!'

Everyone was laughing at my mistake. My face was red!

2 Choose the best title

A funny shopping trip

A horrible shopping trip

A boring shopping trip

3 Do it together

→ Teacher's Book page P18

Where did David go shopping?

He went shopping at the market.

1 **Look at picture A and answer the questions**

1 What winter holiday is it?

2 What is the woman in the orange coat buying?

3 Who is going to get a new coat?

4 What is the man in the blue jacket buying?

5 How many people are having cake?

6 What is the little boy giving the ducks?

2 **Look at picture B and say the differences**

In picture A, the woman in the orange coat is buying chocolate biscuits. In picture B, she's buying sugar.

3 **Questionnaire: talking about food**

fruit   salt
snacks   biscuits
sugar   butter
cake

When you want a snack, do you eat an apple or a biscuit?

A biscuit.

1 Talk about the pictures

Making a cake

4 **Two hours later**

2 Answer the questions

1. What were Helen and Katy doing in the kitchen?

2. What did they take from the cupboard and the fridge?

3. What did Katy do with the eggs and flour?

4. What did they do for two hours?

5. What happened to the cake?

3 Continue the story

Helen and Katy decided to make a cake.

1 Listen, point and say 🎧 28

cheese

meat

restaurant

sandwiches

stomach

2 Read and choose the correct word from above

DAILY NEWS

This is Sonya Thomas. On 1st February, 2006, she won the World Cheese Eating Competition in a New York restaurant. She ate 26 **1** .... sandwiches in ten minutes! The person who came second ate 25½ **2** .... Sonya puts water on her sandwiches. It makes them easier to eat. She says she has a big **3** .... !

After the competition, she had to leave quickly to take a train to her job. She works in a burger **4** .... Sonya has also won other eating competitions. In one competition, she ate 56 burgers in eight minutes. That's a lot of **5** .... !

GOLDEN PALA
.COM
RGIN MARY GRILLED CHEESE

3 Read and choose the correct words

I can eat 100 burgers in three minutes.

1 Sonya Thomas won a competition for eating **a lot/a little**.

2 She ate **half a/a few** sandwich(es) more than the man who came second.

3 **Both/One** of them ate more than 24 sandwiches.

4 If you drink water with bread, it's **easier/harder** to eat.

5 She also ate **a few/a lot of** burgers in a different competition.

1 **Read and find out. Answer the questions.**

1 How long is the New Year holiday in China?

2 Name two ways people get ready for this holiday.

3 What present do children get at this time?

Flying visit: China

Name: Li
Age: 12
Country: China

My name is Li. I'm from China. My favourite holiday is our New Year. This holiday is quite long in China – fifteen days, in January and February.

We do lots of things to get ready for New Year. We clean and paint our houses, and buy new clothes. We wear red because red brings us good things in the future. We visit people and give them oranges. There is a big lion dance in the street. It's fun and exciting.

In the evening before the New Year starts, we eat party food at home with our families. We eat fish, chicken and vegetables. My favourite food is hot rice soup. In China we eat with chopsticks but we eat our soup with a spoon!

On New Year's day, children get red envelopes with money inside. On the last day of the holiday, we have a party in the street with music and dancing. The street is full of little lamps and we eat sweets made of rice flour.

2 **Make sentences about Li and his favourite holiday**

1 Li's favourite holiday is …

2 It's in …

3 During this holiday, people wear …

4 They eat …

5 His favourite food is …

What do you do at New Year?

1 Listen and read 🎧 29

Grandma had a letter to post. She asked David and Helen, 'Can you post this letter for me, please?'

'Of course, Grandma,' said Helen, 'but I don't know the way to the post office.'

'It's easy,' said Grandma. 'Go left, and at the end of the street, turn right. Go straight on, and at the corner, turn left. There are lots of shops in that street. The post office is on the right, next to the bank.'

'Oh, dear. I've forgotten where to go next,' said David.

'I think Grandma said we should turn left at the end of the street,' said Helen.

They turned left, then they went straight on, and at the corner they turned left into Green Street. But there wasn't a post office there, or a bank, and there weren't any shops.

Helen said, 'I think we should go back and start again. Perhaps we should turn right at the end of Grandma's street, not left.'

'We're here!' said Helen. But David looked unhappy.

'I've forgotten the letter!' he said.

2 Read and say *yes* or *no*

1 David and Helen knew the way to the post office.

2 They turned left when they left the house.

3 Grandma told them to turn right at the end of the street.

4 The post office was in Green Street.

5 There weren't any shops in Green Street.

6 The post office was opposite the bank.

I always know the way.

LESSON 2

1 Complete the sentences

1 David and Helen were going to ....

2 At the end of the street, they had to ....

3 They forgot .... to go.

4 The post office is on the right next ....

5 There weren't any shops in ....

6 David forgot ....

There's the post office.

2 Listen and order the cards 🎧 30

➡ Teacher's Book page P19

a Turn left

b Turn right

c Go straight on

d at the corner

e at the end

f on the left

g on the right

h post office

3 Ask and answer together

1 How do you get from your house to school?

2 How do you get from your house to your friend's house?

3 What's opposite your house?

4 Where's the nearest bus stop or station?

5 How do you get from your school to the park?

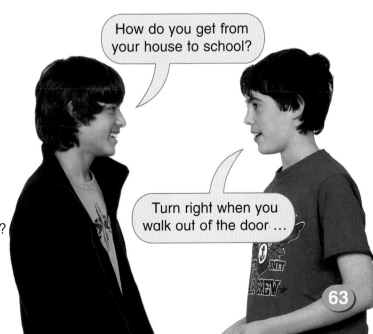

How do you get from your house to school?

Turn right when you walk out of the door …

63

1 **Look and listen. Then answer.** 🎧 31

1 Where are the people going who are getting off the bus?

2 Where's the woman going with her son?

3 Where's the flag?

4 Where's the museum?

5 What was William North's job?

2 **Memory game. Work with a partner.**
Partner A, close your book. Partner B, ask questions.

1 Read and order the pictures

Two men stole a car. They drove away down the street. They drove fast, because the policemen were trying to catch them.

They turned left into a wood and drove through the trees. Then they drove across a bridge. After a few kilometres, they were in a different town. They were lost. They wanted to go home.

So they stopped and asked a man the way to their town. But he was a policeman! They didn't know, because he wasn't wearing a uniform. He said, 'Oh, I was looking for you! The policemen in the other town told me all about you!' So the policeman took them to the police station.

2 Choose the best title

The policeman's mistake

Don't steal!

A policeman loses his way

3 Do it together

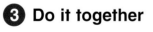 ➡ Teacher's Book page P20

Where's Katy going to go first?

She's going to go across the bridge.

1 **Look at picture A and answer the questions**

1 Where's the post office?

2 What's in the park?

3 Where's the supermarket?

4 Where's the bookshop?

5 What's at the end of Queen Street?

6 Where's the bus?

2 **Look at picture B and say the differences**

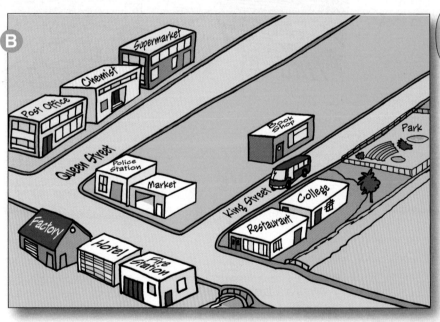

In picture A, the park is in Queen Street. In picture B, the park is in King Street.

3 **Guessing game. Look at picture A.**

I'm between the bank and the chemist.

Are you at the supermarket?

Yes, I am.

LESSON 6

1 **Talk about the pictures**

Finding the way

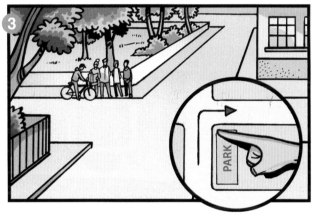

2 **Answer the questions**

1 Which building were David and his family standing in front of?

2 Where did the man tell them to turn?

3 What did the woman tell them to do?

4 What did they do when they came to the corner of the park?

5 What did they find at the end of the street?

3 **Continue the story**

David and his family went to London. They wanted to go to …

1 **Listen, point and say** 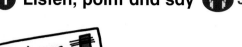 32

address

window

computer

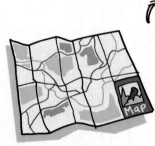

map

turn on

2 **Read and choose the correct word from above**

A few years ago, engineers made a new ⓵ .... for cars. This computer can tell you the way to places. You can put the computer on the front ⓶ .... of your car. When you start driving, you ⓷ .... the computer. If you put in the ⓸ .... it gives you directions. A voice in the computer begins to speak. It tells you when to turn right or left, and when to go straight on.

But you must listen carefully or you can go the wrong way. It knows when you have made a mistake, and tells you to go back again! It's very easy to find your way with this computer. You don't have to have a ⓹ ....!

3 **Read and choose the correct words**

The computer says turn right here!

1 Engineers made the new **computer/map** for cars.

2 It tells you the **address/way**.

3 You have to **turn off/turn on** the computer first.

4 You **must/mustn't** listen to the voice on the computer.

5 You **need/don't need** a map in a car with this computer.

LESSON 8

1 Read and find out. Answer the questions.

1 Where can you find crocodiles and snakes?
2 How many islands are there along the coast in eastern Australia?
3 Where are the best cities?

Flying visit: Australia

Name: Mandy
Age: 12
Country: Australia

Hi! My name's Mandy and I live in Australia. It's a very big country, and each part is different!

But I think the south east where I live, is the most beautiful. It's full of lovely beaches, forests and hills. It's a good place for fishing, with all its rivers and waterfalls. The best cities are here, too!

In the north of the country there are big deserts with red sand, where crocodiles, snakes and other animals like kangaroos live.

The west of Australia is famous for its beaches and sunny weather. People visit this part of the country for swimming, sailing and other water sports. The winters here are cool and the summers are very hot. You can see dolphins and sharks in the sea here.

There are 28 islands along the coast in eastern Australia. In the north east, there are jungles where lots of different parrots and monkeys live.

2 Make sentences about Mandy and her country

1 In the north, there are …
2 In the west, it's famous for …
3 In the west, you can see …
4 In the north east, …
5 She lives in the …, where there are …

Where are the best cities in your country?

1 Listen and read 🎧 33

Katy was looking into her silver ball. Robert wanted to find out about his future.

'Will I do well in my exams this year?' he asked.

Katy looked into the ball. 'Mmm, yes, you may. But you'll have to study for them!'

Then Robert asked another question. 'Will I be rich one day?'

Katy looked carefully. 'I can see you in my silver ball. You're looking at an expensive car.'

Robert was happy. He thought, 'Perhaps I'll be an important businessman.' 'Will I buy the car?' he asked.

'No, you won't,' said Katy. 'I think it's broken. You might be a mechanic.'

Robert didn't mind. He likes cars.

He asked another question. 'Will I travel around the world one day?'

Katy saw a picture of Robert in her silver ball. He was travelling to space in a rocket! 'Well, perhaps you won't be a mechanic. Perhaps you'll be an astronaut, and travel to planets where no-one has ever been!'

'That sounds exciting! How long will I stay there?' asked Robert.

'I don't know. Maybe you won't come back,' answered Katy.

Then Robert said, 'I think I'd prefer to be a mechanic …'

2 Read and say *yes* or *no*

1 Robert may do well in his exams.

2 He won't buy an expensive car.

3 He might be a mechanic one day.

4 He hates cars.

5 He won't travel to space in a rocket.

6 He doesn't want to stay in space for a long time.

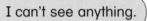
I can't see anything.

I want to be an astronaut.

1 Complete the sentences

1 Katy was ....
2 Robert may pass ....
3 Robert will have to ....
4 Robert won't buy ....
5 Robert will travel ....
6 Robert would prefer ....

2 Listen and order the cards. 🎧 34

➡ Teacher's Book page P21

3 Ask and answer together

Will I work in an office one day?

No, you won't.

1 Will I work in an office one day?
2 Will I be famous?
3 Will I be rich?
4 Where will I live?
5 Where will I travel?

1 **Look and listen. Then answer.** 🎧 35

1 What is this place?

2 Will the dog jump in the lake? Why? Why not?

3 What will the little girl do then?

4 Who will tell the girls the way?

5 Will the man leave the café soon? Why? Why not?

2 **Memory game. Work with a partner.**
Partner A, close your book. Partner B, ask questions.

Why...?

Where's the man who's reading a newspaper?

Where...?

What...?

At the café.

What colour...?

How many...?

Who...?

LESSON 4

1 Read and order the pictures

My mother is a businesswoman. She flies all over the world for business.

Today she is going to China. She'll get on the plane at 7.00 a.m. and she'll arrive in China at 2.00 p.m. the next day!

I think she'll go to her hotel first. Perhaps she'll read some papers for work.

Then she'll have dinner. In China it's seven hours later than it is in England. So if it's dinner time there, it's lunch time here! When Mum goes to bed, I come home. And when she goes to work in the morning, I go to bed!

2 Choose the best title

What I'll have for dinner

The job I'll do one day

Different times around the world

3 Do it together

➡ Teacher's Book page P22

Where's Sarah going to go?

She's going to go to Australia.

1 **Look at picture A. Then look at picture B and answer the questions.**

1 Will there be lots of trees in towns in the future?

2 Will people drive cars in town?

3 Will there be robots?

4 Will people live in houses?

5 How will we travel around town?

A **The past**

2 **Look at pictures A then picture B. Then say the differences between the past and the future.**

B **The future**

In the past, people drove cars in town. In the future, people won't drive cars in town.

3 **Questionnaire: talking about the future**

Cars.

People won't drive cars in town.

houses
robots   cars
trees   rockets
buses

1 Talk about the pictures

Don't dream about the future!

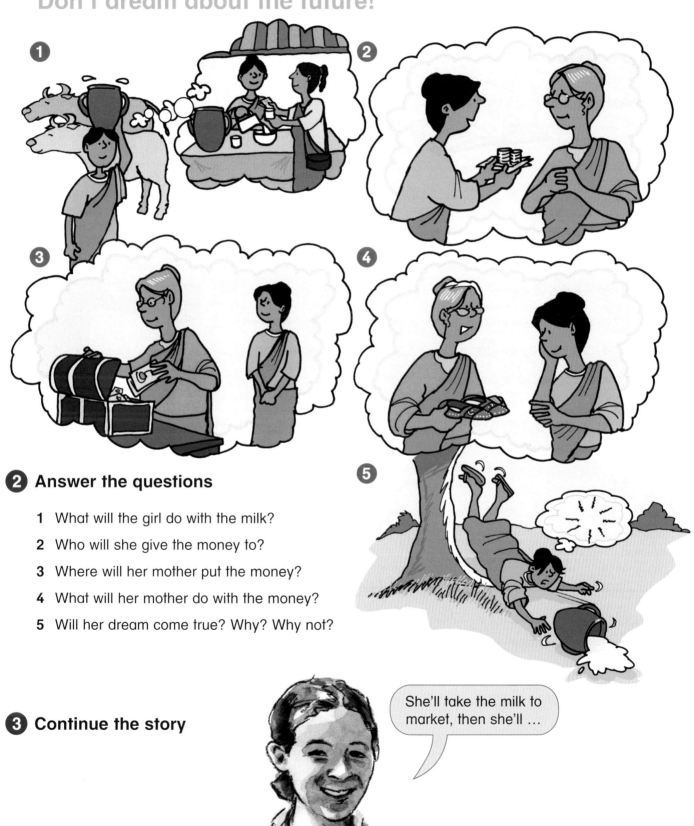

2 Answer the questions

1 What will the girl do with the milk?

2 Who will she give the money to?

3 Where will her mother put the money?

4 What will her mother do with the money?

5 Will her dream come true? Why? Why not?

3 Continue the story

> She'll take the milk to market, then she'll …

1 Listen, point and say 🎧 36

bookshops

page

paper

pocket

shelf

2 Read and choose the correct words from above

What will the world be like in fifty years' time? Will everything be different or just the same? Some people believe that we won't read books made of **1** .... any more. They think all our books will be on computers.

To read, we will turn on the computer, which will be small enough to carry in our **2** .... To turn over to the next **3** .... , we will have to speak to the computer. There won't be **4** .... We will tell the computer the name of the book we want, and then it will copy the book for us. After a few minutes, the book will be on our own computers.

I don't think I'll enjoy reading this way. I don't mind computers, but I like to see my books on a **5** .... !

3 Read and choose the correct words

> I don't know where to put my book.

1 In the future, books will be **different/the same**.

2 Books **will/won't** be made of paper.

3 We will carry new, small computers in our **bookshops/pockets**.

4 We **will/won't** use a computer to buy our books.

5 We **will/won't** see books on shelves.

1 **Read and find out. Answer the questions.**

1 Where was Lily's first home?

2 What are her parents' jobs?

3 Where is she going to live?

Flying visit: Singapore

Name: Lily
Age: 12
Country: Canada

In a few months, my parents will start new jobs in Singapore, so we'll have to move again soon. I don't mind, because it's interesting to learn new things. I'll have to learn to eat with chopsticks, and to speak a new language! When I first arrive, I won't know anybody. But I'll soon make new friends, and they'll help me.

I hate saying goodbye to people. I will be very sad to leave them, because I know I won't see them for a long time. But perhaps they will come and visit me in my new home.

Hi, my name's Lily. My father is a businessman, and my mother is a businesswoman. Their business has offices in lots of different countries, so I have lived all over the world. Our first home was in Canada, but we have lived in the north, west, south and east of the world! At the moment, we are living in London.

And one day, when I leave school, perhaps I will become an important businesswoman, too. Then I will travel all over the world. That way, I will always see my old friends!

2 **Make sentences about Lily and her future**

1 Lily's first home was …

2 Now she lives …

3 Soon she will have to …

4 Lily thinks it's interesting …

5 Lily hates … because …

6 One day, she …

Where will you live one day?

The past, present and future

1 Listen and read 🎧 37

Mr Jones: Welcome to Question Time! Today, we're asking our team questions about the past, the present and the future. OK, the first question is about the past. Katy, a question for you: do you know a lot about dinosaurs?

Katy: I know they are extinct!

Mr Jones: But do you know how big the biggest dinosaur was?

Katy: Er … about 10 metres tall?

Mr Jones: No, sorry! It was much bigger. It was 18 metres tall!

Katy: Oh!

Mr Jones: David, who had the first telephone conversation?

David: He was called Bell. He made the first telephone in 1876.

Mr Jones: Yes, that's right. Now some questions about the world around us today. Helen, which is the biggest water bird in this country?

Helen: The swan?

Mr Jones: Yes. Robert, how many legs has a butterfly got?

Robert: A butterfly … it's an insect, and all insects have got six legs.

Mr Jones: Good. Harry, have baby lions got spots or stripes on their fur?

Harry: Umm, baby lions have got spots.

Mr Jones: Right! And finally, a question about the future. How old will I be next year?

Robert: Sixty-eight?

Katy: Thirty-five?

Mr Jones: I prefer your answer, Katy. You win!

2 Read and say *yes* or *no*

1 Dinosaurs are extinct now.

2 People were already using telephones in 1800.

3 A swan likes to live on water.

4 A butterfly has got six legs.

5 Robert knows how old Mr Jones will be next year.

6 Robert won the competition.

My best friend is a swan.

LESSON 2

> You're 18 metres tall.

1 Complete the sentences

1 Mr Jones .... questions about the past, present and future.

2 The biggest dinosaur .... 18 metres tall.

3 Bell had the first .... in 1876.

4 People .... telephones 200 years ago.

5 Baby lions .... on their fur.

6 A butterfly .... wings.

2 Listen and order the cards 38

→ Teacher's Book page P23

a

b

c

d

e

f

g

h

3 Ask and answer together

1 Are you good at crosswords?

2 How many insects can you name?

3 Have you ever seen a black swan?

4 How can you have 'conversations' on a computer?

5 Do you often phone your friends, or do you prefer to text them?

> Are you good at crosswords?

> No, I'm not.

UNIT 10

1 **Look and listen. Then answer.** 🎧 39

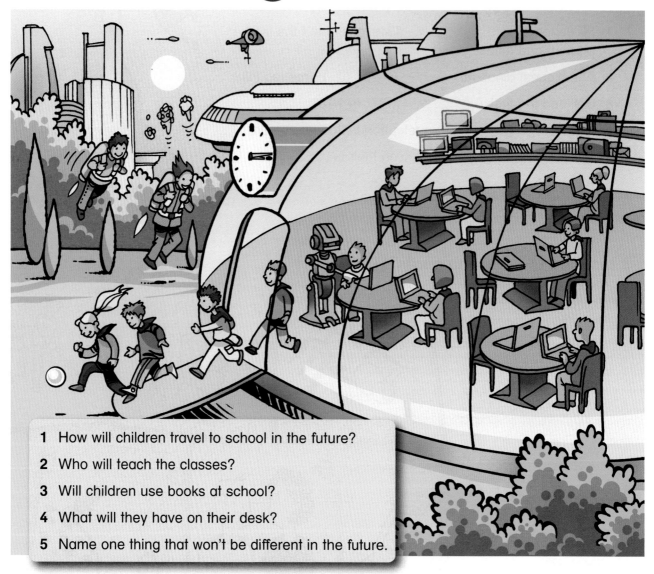

1 How will children travel to school in the future?

2 Who will teach the classes?

3 Will children use books at school?

4 What will they have on their desk?

5 Name one thing that won't be different in the future.

2 **Memory game. Work with a partner.**
Partner A, close your book. Partner B, ask questions.

What time...?

What...?

How many...?

How many children are working at their desks?

Seven.

Where...?

What colour...?

Who...?

1 Read and order the pictures

Today, our class went to the science museum. It was really interesting. We learnt about dinosaurs. They lived many years ago, but now they are extinct.

Then we went to the insect room. I've never seen so many butterflies before! Most had spots or stripes on their wings, and the glass butterfly had wings like glass. You could see through the wings!

The space room was my favourite. We saw rockets and the clothes astronauts wear. But museums aren't only about the past. We also saw ideas for the future. One idea was a robot that could do jobs in the house. I want one like that, to tidy my room!

2 Choose the best title

A day in the past

A day in space

An interesting day

3 Do it together

➡ Teacher's Book page P24

Where did Harry's class go?

They went to the history museum.

❶ Look at picture A and answer the questions

1 Was it summer or winter?

2 What clothes did people wear?

3 Where were the swans?

4 Where did people meet their friends?

5 Were there any planes?

❷ Look at picture B and say the differences

In picture A, people are wearing long coats and hats. In picture B, people are wearing jeans and T-shirts.

❸ Questionnaire: *When did you first … ?*

➡ Teacher's Book page P25

ride   buy
go   see   read
watch   hear
learn   eat

When did you first read a book?

When I was six years old.

1 Talk about the pictures

Treasure from the past

2 Answer the questions

1 What place was David's class visiting?

2 What happened to David?

3 What did he find?

4 What did he do with it?

5 How did David feel at the end of the story?

3 Continue the story

One day, David and his class were visiting ...

1 Listen, point and say 🎧 40

trees

dinosaur

wings

museum

robot

2 Read and choose the correct word from above

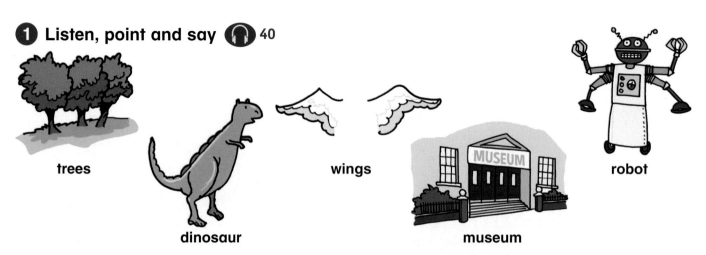

A visit to the ①................... room at the Natural History
②................... in London is very exciting! There's a lot to find out
about these animals that lived a very very long time ago. They are now
extinct, but in the museum, it feels like they are living in the room!
There is one dinosaur that is a ③................... . It sounds and
moves just like a real dinosaur. You can watch it 'eating' a small animal.

The dinosaur in this photo looks very angry, but it only used its teeth to
eat plants and leaves. It didn't eat meat.

Some dinosaurs could fly! People who study dinosaurs believe that these dinosaurs lived in
④................... and had ⑤..................., just like birds. So are birds part of the
dinosaur family? It's an interesting idea!

Do I look like a dinosaur?

3 Read and choose the correct words

1 Dinosaurs **lived/are living** a long time ago.

2 They **are/look like they are** living in the museum today.

3 They **made/were making** a dinosaur into a robot.

4 Some dinosaurs **ate/eat** only plants, not meat.

5 Some people believe that birds **might be/will be** part of
the dinosaur family.

1 **Read and find out. Answer the questions.**

1 How cold is it in winter in Greenland?

2 How many hours a day does the sun shine in summer?

3 Name three things that were different for people in Greenland long ago.

Flying visit: Greenland

Name: Robert
Age: 11
Country:
Greenland

Hi, my name's Robert. I live in Greenland. Greenland is an island to the north east of Canada. People think it's always winter in Greenland. It's true we have winter for about nine months, when the temperature is sometimes −40°C! But we have warm summers, too. In July, the sun shines for about 20 hours a day.

Lots of things have changed for our people. Long ago, we lived in houses made of ice. But today, our houses are made of wood. We don't catch animals for food anymore. We buy most of our food in supermarkets, just like in most other countries! Even our clothes are different. We don't wear animal fur any more. My favourite clothes are jeans and a T-shirt.

In the past, we travelled on sledges. We used dogs to pull the sledges. But now we have motorbikes with skis on them, to help us drive in snow.

The weather around the world is getting warmer all the time. What will happen to Greenland in the future? Nobody knows, but I think it will be very different in 50 years' time.

2 **Make sentences about Robert and his country**

1 His country is an island to the …

2 The winter is …

3 People in his country live in …

4 Robert's favourite clothes are …

5 They drive …

What are winters like in your country?

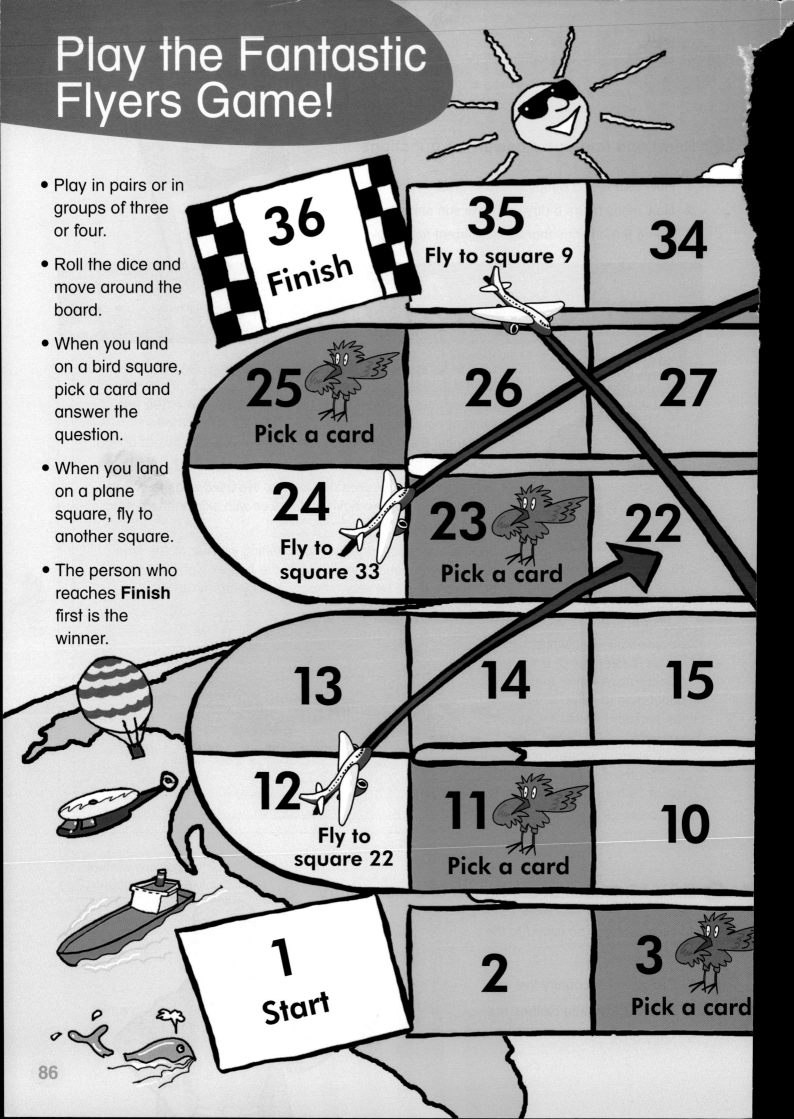

Play the Fantastic Flyers Game!

- Play in pairs or in groups of three or four.
- Roll the dice and move around the board.
- When you land on a bird square, pick a card and answer the question.
- When you land on a plane square, fly to another square.
- The person who reaches **Finish** first is the winner.

36 Finish

35 Fly to square 9

34

25 Pick a card

26

27

24 Fly to square 33

23 Pick a card

22

13

14

15

12 Fly to square 22

11 Pick a card

10

1 Start

2

3 Pick a card